american
MUSIC MILESTONES

AMERICAN Country

BLUEGRASS, HONKY-TONK, AND CROSSOVER SOUNDS

LLOYD SACHS

TFCB
TWENTY-FIRST CENTURY BOOKS
MINNEAPOLIS

NOTE TO READERS: some songs and music videos by artists discussed in this book contain language and images that readers may consider offensive.

Twenty-First Century Books
A division of Lerner Publishing Group, Inc.
241 First Avenue North
Minneapolis, MN 55401 U.S.A.

Website address: www.lernerbooks.com

Library of Congress Cataloging-in-Publication Data

Sachs, Lloyd.
    American country : bluegrass, honky-tonk, and crossover sounds / by Lloyd Sachs.
       pages   cm. — (American music milestones)
    Includes bibliographical references and index.
    ISBN 978–0–7613–4502–2 (lib. bdg. : alk. paper)
    1. Country music—History and criticism—Juvenile literature. I. Title.
  ML3524.S23 2013
  781.6420973—dc23   2011048799

Manufactured in the United States of America
1 – CG – 7/15/12

CONTENTS

chapter 1

Country

STARTS HERE

Country music features different styles and attitudes. Kenny Chesney is one of the most popular acts in country music.

LIKE THE UNITED STATES ITSELF, THE LANDSCAPE OF COUNTRY MUSIC IS SPACIOUS AND VARIED.

A country song can be about anything or anyone. It can be funny, sad, angry, or inspiring. It can stomp like the rock music or swing like jazz. A country singer can look like your favorite uncle or your kid sister, the head cheerleader or the class clown.

Since the start of the twentieth century, country has offered listeners many sounds to choose from. From bluegrass to country rock, from early hero Jimmie Rodgers to Kenny Chesney, the music features different styles and attitudes. Country songs have also reflected times of change in U.S. history.

In the early 1900s, early forms of country known as hillbilly music and mountain music sprang up in the American South. The music had its roots in the folk songs that immigrants brought to the United States from England, Scotland, and Ireland. For many years this music remained in the South. Musicians from states such as Virginia and Kentucky performed songs for their friends and neighbors. That began to change when northern talent scouts traveled to the South in the 1920s and the 1930s to record

Jimmie Rodgers, pictured here in 1930, shaped the sound of country music in the 1920s and the 1930s.

southern artists. For the first time, people in other parts of the country were able to hear southern voices on the radio. The most famous of these talent scouts was Ralph Peer, who worked for the Okeh and Victor record labels. One of Peer's greatest discoveries was Jimmie Rodgers.

JIMMIE RODGERS LIVES!

Jimmie Rodgers has been called the Father of Modern Country. A charming performer, he became

country music's first superstar. Rodgers could make any kind of music his own. He invented the expressive blue yodel by adding his bluesy vocals to the yodel. To yodel, a singer switches between low and very high notes. This way of singing originally came from sheepherders in the mountains of Switzerland.

Rodgers was born in Mississippi in 1897. As a young man he worked on railroad lines. Traveling across the South, he absorbed its different cultures. The blues music of African Americans made a strong impression on him. In fact, some people consider his song "Blue Yodel No. 1" (1928) to be the first example of white blues.

Rodgers had a gift for shaping his image. He appeared in film shorts wearing overalls and a cap. In this outfit, he played a working-class character called the Singing Brakeman. These shorts played in movie theaters in the 1930s. They were the closest thing to music videos at the time. Rodgers could also present himself as an elegant gentleman. He often performed in a suit and bow tie. He could be anyone his audience wanted him to be.

Listeners can't fully understand where country comes from without noting the mark Rodgers left on it. Songs such as "In the Jailhouse Now" (1928) and "Muleskinner Blues" (1931) shaped the music that followed them. Fans can only imagine the impact Rodgers would have made if he had not died young. He passed away from tuberculosis at the age of thirty-five.

COUNTRY'S FIRST FAMILY

Modern country music also points back to the Carter Family. This band came out of Virginia's Clinch Mountains in the late 1920s. The Clinch Mountains was a place of awesome natural beauty but also of economic hardship. Music was one way people who lived there fought the sorrow of poverty. Carter Family recordings such as "Wildwood Flower" (1928) and "Can the Circle Be Unbroken" (1935) have never lost their power.

The Carters were a three-piece group. The moody A. P. Carter wrote the songs. He sang with a deep bass voice. His wife, Sara Carter, sang lead. A.P.'s sister-in-law, Maybelle Carter, gave the music a special bounce

Maybelle Carter LEFT, A. P. Carter MIDDLE, and Sara Carter RIGHT rose out of rural Virginia playing powerful mountain music.

HERE a CARTER, THERE a CARTER

After the **Carter Family** called it quits, **Maybelle Carter** began to perform with her three daughters, **Helen, Anita, and June** (ABOVE). June later married country singer **Johnny Cash**. In the 1980s the Carter sisters and June's daughter **Carlene** formed a new version of the Carter Family. The Carters still contribute to country music. June's stepdaughter is the modern singer-songwriter **Rosanne Cash**. Rosanne dedicates herself to continuing what A.P., Sara, and Maybelle started. **John Carter Cash** is the grandson of Maybelle and the son of Johnny Cash and June. John works as a producer and a singer-songwriter.

with her unique "scratching" guitar style. With this style, she could play a song's melody and its rhythm at the same time.

The Carters's vocal harmonies and playing had a solemn, God-fearing intensity. Their fame took them to Texas and North Carolina, where they hosted popular live radio programs. In 1941 A.P. and Sara split up. The Carter Family stopped making records. That year, the Japanese military bombed the American naval base at Pearl Harbor in Hawaii. The bombing led the United States to fight in World War II (1939–1945). The Carters and other hillbilly musicians suddenly seemed old fashioned.

MILLION-SELLING MONTANA

Patsy Montana (Ruby Blevins) was a fiddling and yodeling cowgirl from Arkansas. She was also one of country music's first female session musicians. (Session musicians play on the studio recordings of other artists.) Montana added violin sounds to 1932 recordings by Jimmie Davis, a future governor of Louisiana.

Montana was known as the Girl with the Million-Dollar Personality.

FDR, BABE RUTH, and ROY

Just how famous was **Roy Acuff**? According to World War II lore, he was one of three American heroes singled out in 1945 by Japanese fighter pilots. Before their attack on U.S. troops in the Pacific, the pilots were said to have cried, "To hell with [U.S. president **Franklin Delano] Roosevelt**! To hell with [baseball great] **Babe Ruth**! To hell with Roy Acuff!"

Four years earlier, Acuff had performed "Cowards over Pearl Harbor" (1941). His business partner Fred Rose wrote the song after Japan's surprise attack on Pearl Harbor. During this era, many popular entertainers saw it as their duty to mock Japan and other wartime enemies of the United States.

In 1933 she visited the Chicago World's Fair. During a singing audition at the fair, she charmed a producer from Chicago's WLS radio station. He hired her as the featured singer on the station's popular *National Barn Dance* program. In 1935 Montana became the first woman in country music to sell one million copies of a record with the peppy "I Want to Be a Cowboy's Sweetheart." With later songs such as "I Only Want a Buddy, Not a Sweetheart" (1937), she showed a confidence and sense of independence that inspired later generations of female country singers.

Montana later appeared in the film *Colorado Sunset* (1939) with singing cowboy Gene Autry. With her band, the Prairie Ramblers, she remained the star attraction of *National Barn Dance* until 1952.

Patsy Montana smiles for the camera in 1970. Montana was country's first female solo star.

THE WAR YEARS

World War II created many factory jobs in U.S. cities such as Chicago, Detroit, and Baltimore. The promise of work drew many southerners to the North. These new workers brought their culture with them. Meanwhile, many northern soldiers at military bases in the South discovered country music.

During the war, country artists began recording songs that all kinds of listeners, not just southerners, could relate to. Soon California's singing cowboys Gene Autry and Roy Rogers became stars on records and in the movies and later on TV. Popular crooners such as Bing Crosby brought a touch of humor

OPRY MUSIC

If you're wondering what the heck an *opry* is, don't look in the dictionary. The word became part of country slang in 1927. **George Hay** was the host and producer of Nashville's weekly WSM *Barn Dance* radio show. This show put live country performances on the air. Hay's show came after a classical music program called *The Music Appreciation Hour*. One Saturday night, Hay told listeners that after listening to opera music on the *Appreciation Hour*, it was time to listen to some "grand ole opry" on his show. Hay's remark became the program's new name. It also became the name of the different concert venues that have been the program's home. For country artists, an invitation to play the Opry is still an honor.

I was stubborn and opinionated in everything…from business to politics. Because if you aren't, you got no vision, and who needs you?

—Roy Acuff, n.d.

to country music. Crosby recorded chart-topping country songs such as "Sioux City Sue" (1946).

Some people saw these new forms of country as a threat to the mountain music they loved. These people found their champion in Roy Acuff, Tennessee's King of Country. This singer and fiddler was committed to old-time melodies and sacred (religious) songs. Acuff's group, the Smoky Mountain Boys, stuck with a traditional mountain-music lineup of fiddle, string bass, rhythm guitar, and banjo.

Acuff poured so much emotion into songs of faith such as "Great Speckled Bird" (1936) that he sometimes wept at the microphone. He became the first great singing star of *The Grand Ole Opry*. The Opry is a beloved radio program that started on station WSM in Nashville, Tennessee, in the 1920s.

Roy Acuff SECOND FROM LEFT, performing here in 1943, wasn't just an influential country musician. He changed the business of country music too.

ACUFF-ROSE

Roy Acuff helped shape country music as a businessperson. In 1942 he and Chicago songwriter Fred Rose formed the first music-publishing house in Nashville: Acuff-Rose Publications, Inc. Companies like these worked to make sure that songwriters received fair payment when their works were played live or aired on the radio. In the past, many country artists had been cheated by agents, record labels, and record promoters. Acuff-Rose brought about major changes for country artists by signing with Broadcast Music, Inc. (BMI). BMI became the first company to collect performance royalties (payments) for country songwriters.

Until 1940 the powerful New York–based American Society of Composers, Authors and Publishers (ASCAP) was the only major agency to collect performance royalties. The ASCAP shut out country artists and concentrated on pop music. But a series of hits from Acuff-Rose artists proved that traditional country could be big business. As a result, more record companies devoted themselves to country. The music prospered in the years after World War II ended. ★

MUST DOWNLOAD
Playlist

UNCLE DAVE MACON,
"Hill Billie Blues" (1924)

CHARLIE POOLE,
"Don't Let Your Deal Go Down Blues" (1925)

CARTER FAMILY,
"Wildwood Flower" (1928)

JIMMIE RODGERS,
"Blue Yodel No. 1" (1928)

PATSY MONTANA,
"I Want to Be a Cowboy's Sweetheart" (1935)

ROY ACUFF,
"Great Speckled Bird" (1936)

WOODY GUTHRIE,
"Do Re Mi" (1937)

GENE AUTRY,
"Back in the Saddle Again" (1939)

ROY ROGERS AND THE SONS OF THE PIONEERS,
"Blue Shadows on the Trail" (1948)

DELMORE BROTHERS,
"Blues Stay Away from Me" (1950)

chapter 2

ALL Hank BREAKS LOOSE

HANK WILLIAMS'S SONG "HONKY TONKIN'" (1948) MADE THE TERM *HONKY-TONK* FAMOUS.

The term was first used during the Prohibition era (1920–1933). During this time, the manufacture and sale of alcoholic drinks was illegal in the United States. But many places sold alcohol in secret. In Texas, honky-tonks were bars where oil-field workers went to cut loose. Things got wild at these bars. For safety, musicians had to perform behind chicken wire so they weren't hit with flying bottles. The wilder the crowds, the more aggressive the music had to be. Most honky-tonk songs were set in a world of drinking, cheating, lying, and regretting.

One song that fit the bill to a Texas T was the 1943 hit "Pistol Packin' Mama" by Al Dexter (Clarence Albert Poindexter). The song was a humorous number that ended on a violent note. It told the story of a fun-loving but unfaithful man—named Al Dexter—who is shot by his lover.

Honky-tonk dominated country music in the mid-1940s. The rowdy style gave fans such great artists as Floyd Tillman

Al Dexter STANDING CENTER, pictured here in 1943, wrote the humorous hit "Pistol Packin' Mama."

Hank Williams goes honky-tonkin' in 1951.

Lefty Frizzell led a troubled life, but he left behind numerous beloved songs including "Always Late" and "Travelin' Blues" (1951).

problem led to his early death at the age of forty-seven.

MAKE IT SWING

Bob Wills is another figure from the 1930s and the 1940s who made a lasting impact on country music. He and His Texas Playboys were known for a style called Western swing. Western hints at the music's cowboy touches. Swing refers to its bouncy, side-to-side feel. Jazz bandleaders such as Benny Goodman first made the sound and style of swing famous in the 1930s. Young people danced to the music with energetic tosses, spins, and dips.

Wills, from eastern Texas, didn't invent Western swing. Bandleaders including Milton Brown and Roy Newman got there first. But no one spread the gospel of Western swing like Wills and His Texas Playboys. Their songs drew country listeners into dance halls.

Wills was ahead of his time. His band mixed different strains of regional music such as Tex-Mex (from southern Texas), ragtime, and Dixieland (both from New Orleans). It used horns and drums at a time when most country bands shunned these instruments. Wills's independent spirit cost him.

and Ernest Tubb. Tillman is known as the Father of Honky-Tonk. He sang such songs as "I Love You So Much It Hurts" (1947) and "Slippin' Around" (1949). Tubb was a Texas native with a deep, gravelly voice. He gave honky-tonk a wider audience with his 1941 hit "Walking the Floor over You." Tubb was the first electric guitarist to appear at the Grand Ole Opry. And then there was William "Lefty" Frizzell, a stylish Texan with a high voice. Along with Hank Williams, Frizzell was the top hit maker of his era.

Frizzell acquired the nickname Lefty from his days as a boxer. His songs combined the country blues of Jimmie Rodgers and the tough sounds of Texas barroom music. In 1951 Frizzell achieved major success by placing four songs in the Top 10 at the same time: "I Want to Be with You Always," "Always Late," "Mom and Dad's Waltz," and "Travelin' Blues." But the giddy 1950 hit that rocketed him to stardom, "If You've Got the Money I've Got the Time," didn't match his life. Frizzell sometimes skipped concerts and recording sessions. He drank heavily and spent money carelessly. Frizzell's personal problems knocked his career off the rails. His drinking

Bob Wills and His Texas Playboys get ready to hit the road in 1945.

TAKING RISKS, MAKING TREASURE

Through the years, lots of recordings by **Bob Wills and His Texas Playboys** have been available to listeners. But 2008's The Tiffany Transcriptions was a treasure trove of more than 360 never-before-collected songs. Music from the collection was originally recorded in the mid-1940s for the Tiffany Music Company of Oakland, California. The songs were meant to be sold to radio stations as prerecorded shows. The collection captures the band in a freer, jazzier, and riskier spirit than the band's studio recordings.

The Grand Ole Opry didn't support his type of music. Without that support, Wills was never as famous during his lifetime as he deserved to be. But he later became a country music legend.

PUTTING THE BLUE IN BLUEGRASS

Bill Monroe took the name of his band from a type of grass called bluegrass that grew in his home state of Kentucky. Monroe's Blue Grass Boys inspired a whole musical style. The Blue Grass Boys formed in the 1930s. In 1945 breathtaking banjo player Earl Scruggs and guitarist Lester Flatt joined the group. Scruggs's skill added new energy to the Boys' old-time string-based sound.

Monroe sang of tragic love, lonesome pines, log cabins, death, and religion. His high, woeful voice became a trademark of bluegrass. He and the Blue Grass Boys performed new songs as well as traditional tunes, including "I'm a Man of Constant Sorrow" and "I Wonder How the Old Folks Are at Home." In 1948 Scruggs and Flatt formed

Bill Monroe and his band the Blue Grass Boys developed a lasting, string-based sound.

Earl Scruggs SECOND FROM LEFT and Lester Flatt FAR RIGHT play bluegrass with the Foggy Mountain Boys in 1950.

their own bluegrass group, the Foggy Mountain Boys.

Bluegrass was most popular in the early 1950s. But even then there weren't many bands making bluegrass records. Bluegrass greats of this time included Flatt and Scruggs, the Country Gentlemen, and the Stanley Brothers. Throughout the next few decades, different groups of musicians rediscovered bluegrass. For example, in the 1960s, folk singers on the East Coast played bluegrass songs with political messages on the electric guitar.

THE LOVESICK BLUES BOY

Hank Williams is widely thought to be the greatest country artist of all time. Long after his death in 1953, Williams classics such as "I'm So Lonesome I Could Cry" (1949), "Hey, Good Lookin'" (1951), and "Your Cheatin' Heart" (1952) pack as much emotion as ever.

The rail-thin, hollow-cheeked Williams overcame hardship to achieve success. He was born into poverty in rural Alabama, the sickly son of an absent father. He began using alcohol during his early teens. He also began playing at square

dances and hoedowns—and writing songs.

As popular as Williams became in his home state, he was rejected by record labels outside of Alabama. He also had trouble getting an invitation to appear on the Grand Ole Opry. When he finally made it on the Opry in 1952, all Hank broke loose. Williams performed a hurting-from-the-toes cover of "Lovesick Blues," a popular tune from the 1920s. It made him an instant star. No one had ever heard anyone like him. For many listeners, his songs did more than reflect or imitate life. They *were* life.

Williams enjoyed stretches of happiness after becoming a star. He even stopped drinking for a while. But his personal life was messy. His

BLUEGRASS ON-SCREEN

During the 1960s, millions of Americans became bluegrass fans through "The Ballad of Jed Clampett." This ballad was the catchy theme song to *The Beverly Hillbillies*, a TV sitcom (ABOVE). The popular show was about a family of country bumpkins who inherit a fortune and move to Southern California's rich Beverly Hills neighborhood. The tune was a number one country hit in 1963 for **Lester Flatt** and **Earl Scruggs**. Years later, bluegrass got attention again through the film *Deliverance* (1972). In *Deliverance*, city slickers on a rafting trip are terrorized by backwoods dwellers. The film features a mesmerizing musical duel between a guitarist and a banjo player.

wife, Audrey, hoped to be a singer herself. She pushed hard to be a part of his performances. Career pressures made their marriage worse. The two had a painful divorce. Audrey won custody of their son, Hank Jr. Williams remarried, but he began to rely more heavily on alcohol and drugs. At the age of twenty-nine, he died from heart problems made worse by his addiction.

During his brief time as a recording artist, Williams cut sixty-six songs. Sometimes he could knock out three songs in a single day. Amazingly, for every ten he recorded, about seven became hits. ★

" I like to think that folk songs express the hopes and dreams of working people. "

—Hank Williams, 1951

HANK'S RULES

Many music fans consider **Bob Dylan** (ABOVE) **the greatest songwriter of his era. Beginning in the 1960s, Dylan became an inspiration to fans of both folk and rock music. His classic songs include "Blowin' in the Wind" (1963) and "The Times They Are a-Changin'" (1964). In his 2004 memoir,** Chronicles: Volume One, **Dylan wrote that musicians could find the "rules of poetic songwriting" in the songs of** Hank Williams. **In 2011 Dylan released** The Lost Notebooks of Hank Williams. **This album features rock and country greats including Dylan,** Jack White, Norah Jones, **and** Sheryl Crow **singing some of Williams's previously unrecorded lyrics.**

MUST DOWNLOAD Playlist

BOB WILLS AND HIS TEXAS PLAYBOYS,
"Big Beaver" (1940)

ERNEST TUBB,
"Walking the Floor over You" (1941)

FLOYD TILLMAN,
"I Love You So Much It Hurts" (1947)

HANK WILLIAMS,
"Lovesick Blues" (1949)

BILL MONROE AND HIS
BLUE GRASS BOYS,
"Can't You Hear Me Callin'?" (1949)

LEFTY FRIZZELL,
"If You've Got the Money I've Got the Time" (1950)

HANK SNOW,
"I'm Moving On" (1950)

HANK THOMPSON,
"The Wild Side of Life" (1952)

FLATT AND SCRUGGS,
"The Ballad of Jed Clampett" (1962)

ERIC WEISSBERG AND STEVE MANDELL,
"Dueling Banjos" (1972)

NASHVILLE TO Bakersfield

chapter 3

Elvis Presley performs in concert in 1956. Elvis was a rockabilly artist.

IN THE 1950S, THE UNITED STATES WENT THROUGH AN ECONOMIC BOOM.

Many families had more money than ever before. But many teens were restless. They were drawn to the rebellious spirit of rock 'n' roll. Elvis Presley brought this new music to American listeners with his two-sided hit "That's All Right"/"Blue Moon of Kentucky" (1954).

Presley's sexy moves and swaggering songs shocked many Americans. Many grown-ups didn't want their kids listening to the music at all. Television producers even believed that Presley's wild hip movements would upset viewers. During one of Presley's TV appearances on the popular Ed Sullivan Show in 1957, the cameras only filmed him from the waist up. Yet the more adults criticized Presley, the more young people loved him.

Presley was one of many early rock musicians also known as rockabilly artists. Rockabilly—rock crossed with hillbilly—first came out of Memphis, Tennessee's Sun Records. Rockabilly was good-time music that was great for dancing. But it also expressed the frustrations of young southerners. "There was a menacing [scary] air of violence about it," critic John Morthland once wrote. Its most famous performers are Presley, Jerry Lee Lewis, Carl Perkins, Wanda Jackson, and Johnny Cash. These artists put their stamps on country as well as rock music.

Ray Charles FRONT and Johnny Cash BACK play together in 1970 during an episode of The Johnny Cash Show. Johnny Cash collaborated with artists from all different musical genres.

THE MANY MOODS OF JOHNNY CASH

When Johnny Cash died in 2009, he was a humble, soft-spoken man. But as a young man, Cash was a hell-raiser. He spent a lot of time struggling with his rowdy streak. His substance abuse led to several brushes with the law, and he served several stays in jail. However, Cash was able to admit his flaws, and his fans loved him even more for it.

Born in Arkansas, Cash reached the Grand Ole Opry in 1956 on the strength of his big hit from that year, "I Walk the Line." He loomed over the landscape with his songs about trains, prison, and outlaw life. He gained more fans while hosting The Johnny Cash Show (1969–1971). Cash championed young artists such as Bob Dylan and Neil Young on the program.

Known as the Man in Black (for his black outfits), Cash scored a huge hit in 1969 with "A Boy Named Sue." But his record sales dipped in following years. As a result, his longtime label Columbia Records dropped him in 1986.

Johnny Cash, performing here in 1978, was a musical rebel, a crossover star, and a country legend.

His only notable recordings during the eighties were with the High-waymen. This supergroup included country stars Willie Nelson, Way-lon Jennings, and Kris Kristofferson.

In the 1990s, an unlikely ally came to Cash's rescue. Rick Rubin was a long-bearded punk, hip-hop, and rock producer. Rubin made the Man in Black cool to young listen-ers by playing up Cash's bad-boy image. He guided Cash through a series of stripped-down albums that featured cover versions of songs by rock artists such as Tom Petty and U2. In 2002, the year before his death, Cash made a recording of the Nine Inch Nails song "Hurt." It also became a haunting music vid-eo. On Cash's final recordings, his voice is barely more than a croak. But he pours feeling and meaning into every note.

COUNTRY FOR GROWN-UPS

Nashville is the most important place country music has ever known. It's where many country stars live and make records and where country bands perform every night of the year. It's where aspiring artists go to write songs, connect with other singers or songwriters, and sop up inspiration. It's where the Country Music Association, the Country Music Hall of Fame, and the Grand Ole Opry are based.

By the late fifties, some older fans had been driven away from country. They were put off by the hot guitars and snarling vocals of rockabilly. Nashville producers developed a softer sound to at-tract older fans. These softer songs boasted string sections and choirs.

THE QUEEN of COUNTRY

The Nashville-born **Kitty Wells** (ABOVE) is known as the Queen of Country Music. In 1952 Wells released her breakthrough hit, "It Wasn't God Who Made Honky-Tonk Angels." Wells's song, written by Jay Miller, was a response to another 1952 country tune. Hank Thompson's "The Wild Side of Life" blamed "faithless women" for broken relationships. Wells took Thompson to task. She sang about married men who acted as if they were single.

Wells's song was controversial. At that time, country music had little space for challenging women. But "Angels" overcame critics with its catchy melody and bold vocals. It became the first tune by a female country artist to top the Billboard singles chart. The success of "Angels" helped pave the way for outspoken singers such as Loretta Lynn and Dolly Parton.

At the heart of the new Nashville sound was the team of guitarist Chet Atkins, pianist Floyd Cramer, and saxophonist Boots Randolph. Together they played on and produced dozens of recordings. The biggest male star of the Nashville sound was "Gentleman Jim" Reeves. Reeves was loved for the "touch of velvet" in his baritone voice.

Former rockabilly musician Conway Twitty also hit it big with Nashville's new sound. So did Don Gibson, a powerful singer and gifted songwriter. Gibson tunes such as "Sea of Heartbreak" (1961) became hits across musical styles. Blues great B. B. King, soul legend Ray Charles, and rocker Bruce Springsteen have all recorded versions of this song.

COUNTRY ACROSS the WORLD

In the early 1900s, English, Scottish, and Irish immigrants brought their native folk music to the United States. Later on, American country music crossed back over the Atlantic. Country artists became popular in England and other parts of Europe.

Gentleman Jim Reeves (LEFT) was among the artists responsible for bringing country music overseas in the 1960s. Reeves had a string of number one songs in Ireland and England. Hits such as "Four Walls" (1957) and "He'll Have to Go" (1960) established him as a favorite in Europe. Reeves was said to be more popular than Elvis Presley in South Africa. Reeves toured in that country and recorded a series of songs in the Afrikaans language spoken there.

Buck Owens made a splash overseas too. In 1967 he and the Buckaroos toured Japan and recorded a live album there. As a result of the tour, Japanese young adults became interested in country music.

By the 1990s, country music's popularity overseas was slipping. However, country megastar Garth Brooks's world tours were still phenomenal sellers. Recently, Country Music Television has spread country to places such as Scandinavia, Belgium, and the Netherlands.

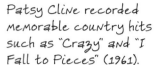
Patsy Cline recorded memorable country hits such as "Crazy" and "I Fall to Pieces" (1961).

PATSY

No Nashvillian had the impact of Patsy Cline. Her charisma and self-reliance made her a true American idol. But Cline changed fans' idea of what women in country could be.

She started out with a string of rowdy releases. Her big break came with the dreamy, swaying song "Walkin' after Midnight" (1957). The song won the top prize on a popular radio show. Cline became the first female singer in country to sell out concert halls without the help of co-billed male stars.

Cline was born Virginia Patterson Hensley in Virginia in 1932. She could drink men under the table, had a chaotic love life, and lived recklessly. Cline's life was rowdy, but her biggest hits, such as "I Fall to Pieces" (1961), were controlled and polished. Legendary producer Owen Bradley recorded Cline in an old barn on a farm outside of Nashville. He brought out her sensitive side on ballads with sobbing strings and backup vocals by the Jordanaires. Cline died in a plane crash in 1963 at the age of thirty-one, only two years after releasing "I Fall to Pieces."

THE REAL LORETTA

Cline was a major inspiration for Loretta Lynn. Lynn fought her way out of an unhappy life in Butcher's Hollow, Kentucky. Listeners didn't get any sense of her feistiness on her early duets with Conway Twitty, including the heartstring-pulling 1958 smash "It's Only Make Believe." But Lynn quickly developed into one of country music's most outspoken, truth-telling artists—and one of its rootsiest singers.

Lynn's songs were cut from the cloth of real life. "Don't Come Home A-Drinkin' (With Lovin' on Your Mind)" (1966) was aimed at Lynn's husband, Moody. "The Pill" (1975) was a frank song about birth control. As with Johnny Cash, Lynn's career sagged after her first years of stardom. But in 2004, she surprised fans by teaming up with Jack White of the White Stripes rock duo. White produced Lynn's

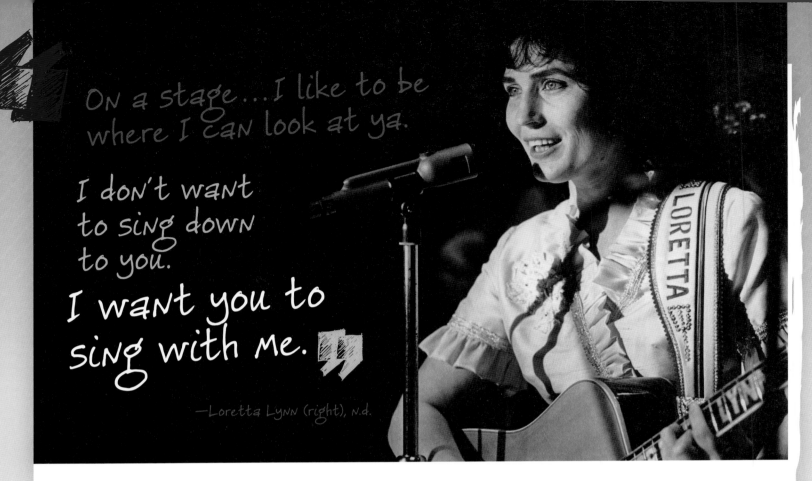

On a stage...I like to be where I can look at ya.

I don't want to sing down to you.

I want you to sing with me.

—Loretta Lynn (right), n.d.

Grammy-winning album **Van Lear Rose**. The record proved to listeners that she hadn't lost any of her edge.

GEORGE AND TAMMY

One artist Nashville could never contain was Texas native George Jones. He stood alone among other country artists because of his remarkable voice. Jones could shift from tender restraint to a clenched wail. He contributed to the success of the Nashville sound with smooth hits such as "Tender Years" (1961). But those songs reflected only one side of his talent. His roots were in honky-tonk, and he was strongly influenced by Hank Williams, Lefty Frizzell, and Bill Monroe.

In addition to one-of-a-kind hits such as "The Race Is On" (1964) and "She Thinks I Still Care" (1962), Jones is known for his duets in the 1960s and the 1970s with his then-wife Tammy Wynette. Wynette was another country star, best known for her song "Stand by Your Man" (1968). The marital troubles of Jones and Wynette were front-page news. Jones struggled with drug and alcohol abuse, and the two fought often. They divorced in 1975, after six years of marriage. However, the couple later patched up their differences and recorded together again. Jones and Wynette stood by each other as friends until Wynette's death in 1998. Jones continues to tour and record.

HELLO, DOLLY

With her mass of platinum hair and giggly laugh, Dolly Parton is an over-the-top figure to many Americans. But Parton's early recordings reveal a thoughtful artist. Albums such as **Coat of Many Colors** (1971) bridged traditional and modern country music. Parton was at home with all kinds of songs. She sang about death, girls gone wrong, religion, and social issues. For example, in "Just Because I'm a Woman" (1968), Parton tells of a cheating husband who wrongly commits his wife to a mental institution.

Parton wrote songs for other artists before she stepped into the spotlight. Then, in 1967, Grand Ole Opry favorite Porter Wagoner asked Parton to join his country television show. Performances on The Porter Wagoner Show and tours with Wagoner launched Parton to country stardom. In the 1970s, she went out on her own. With the million-selling album **Here You Come Again** (1977), Parton became a crossover success, winning over pop-music fans. In 1992 Parton's "I Will Always Love You" (1974) became a smash hit for R & B star Whitney Houston. In the late nineties, Parton returned to her roots with a series of heartfelt, back-to-basics albums.

COUNTRYPOLITAN CALLING

As polished as the Nashville sound could be, an even slicker Nashville style known as countrypolitan sprang up alongside it. (Its name combines *country* with *cosmopolitan*,

Dolly Parton RIGHT become one of the biggest country stars of the 1970s after releasing the album **Here You Come Again** (1977).

Tammy Wynette LEFT and George Jones gained country fame in the 1960s, both for their solo performances and for their electrifying duets.

which means "worldly" or "sophisticated.") Billy Sherrill was the producer behind many countrypolitan songs. The Nashville sound often added string arrangements and big vocal choruses to standard country instruments such as fiddle, Dobro, and steel guitar. But countrypolitan songs used traditional instruments less frequently and sometimes not at all.

Some exceptional musicians were linked to countrypolitan. Charlie Rich recorded catchy hits such as "Behind Closed Doors" (1973) and "The Most Beautiful Girl" (1973). But these songs only began to suggest his strength and range. Countrypolitan's poster boy was the blazer-wearing crooner Eddy Arnold. His smooth vocals had barely a ripple in them. And Crystal Gayle—Loretta Lynn's long-haired little sister—rocketed up the charts in 1977 with the coolly swinging "Don't It Make My Brown Eyes Blue."

COUNTRY, CALIFORNIA STYLE

Beginning in the late 1950s, the California town of Bakersfield produced a no-nonsense, high-energy form of country music. Known as the Bakersfield sound, this

In the 1960s, country's popularity was rising. So singers from pop music invaded Nashville recording studios. Stylish crooner **Dean Martin** was a frequent visitor. He recorded albums such as *Country Style* (1963). It included cover versions of **Hank Williams's** "I'm So Lonesome I Could Cry" and **Johnny Cash's** "I Walk the Line." In 1967 **Nancy Sinatra** (ABOVE), daughter of singer **Frank Sinatra**, recorded *Country, My Way*. The album gave her the Top 10 hit "Jackson," a duet with Lee Hazelwood. And folk-rock singer **Bob Dylan** recorded the album *Nashville Skyline* in 1969 with a crew of local musicians.

special brand of country music has its roots in Oklahoma. During the Great Depression (1929–1942), huge dust storms ruined millions of acres of Oklahoma farmland. The dust forced thousands of "Okies" to leave home. Many went to Bakersfield for jobs in oil fields and on farms, picking fruit and other crops.

The Bakersfield sound was hardedged and relentless. It had to be. Workers needed an escape from their tough lives and hard jobs. They needed music to shout and dance to. Local favorites Tommy Collins and Wynn Stewart filled barrooms with their vocals, shrieking guitars, and crying violins. Even the ballads had an edge.

BUCKING THE MAINSTREAM

The Bakersfield sound hit its peak in the 1960s. Hit after country hit had a West Coast postmark. Along with Collins and Stewart, Collins's onetime guitarist Buck Owens defined the Bakersfield sound. True to his name, the Texas native bucked (rebelled against) the polished sounds coming out of Nashville. His energetic hits included "Under Your Spell Again" (1959) and "Above and Beyond" (1960).

Other musicians recorded hit covers of songs written by Owens and his band, the Buckaroos. Ray Charles scored big with two Owens classics, "Crying Time" (1966) and "Together Again" (1966). And the Beatles' version of the Owens song "Act Naturally" was the B-side of their single "Yesterday" (1965). The artistic spark went out of Owens in 1974. That year his friend and Buckaroos guitarist Don Rich died. "I think my music life ended when [Rich] did . . . the real lightning and thunder is gone forever," Owens once wrote.

At the time of Rich's death, Owens was cohosting *Hee Haw*. He appeared on this popular country TV show from 1969 to 1986. Many people remember Owens mainly for that role. But he is just as

Country fans of the twenty-first century turn to the cable channel Country Music Television (CMT) to watch their favorite singers. But country artists have been on TV for decades. From 1955 to 1960, singer Red Foley hosted the popular Saturday night ABC series *Ozark Jubilee*. (This show was later known as *Country Music Jubilee* and then as *Jubilee USA*.) In the 1960s, Texan Roger Miller (ABOVE RIGHT) hit it big with pop-country songs such as "Dang Me" (1965) and "King of the Road" (1965). Miller hosted a variety show in 1967 on TV's NBC network.

Two years later, *The Glen Campbell Goodtime Hour* premiered on CBS. The show's host, Glen Campbell, was the first singer to win Grammys in both country and pop in the same year. He won for "Gentle on My Mind" (1967) and for "By the Time I Get to Phoenix" (1967). Campbell's strong ratings paved the way for *The Johnny Cash Show* on ABC, as well as for *Pop! Goes the Country* (1974–1982), hosted by songwriter Tom T. Hall.

Country heroes FROM LEFT TO RIGHT: Johnny Cash, Merle Haggard, Buck Owens, and Glen Campbell gather together during a 1975 TV performance.

important for inspiring young country singers and songwriters. For example, Dwight Yoakam expresses his debt to Owens. The two recorded a duet called "Streets of Bakersfield" in 1988. The song became Owens's first number one hit in sixteen years.

MERLE'S BLUES

On April 6, 1937, Merle Haggard was born in a boxcar in Bakersfield. His father, James Haggard, was an Okie railroad worker who had led bands himself. James died suddenly when Merle was nine. Merle took years to recover from the loss. As a teen, Merle was in and out of jail for burglary and other crimes. Married at nineteen, he had five

LIVE at SAN QUENTIN

Merle Haggard first met Johnny Cash in 1958. Twenty-three-year-old Haggard was serving time in San Quentin State Prison in California for armed robbery. That year Cash and his band gave a performance at the California prison. The two men talked about their meeting when Haggard appeared on Cash's TV show in 1968. Haggard recalled the prison concert.

"That's funny, I don't remember you being on that show," said Cash.

"I wasn't," said Haggard. "I was in the audience."

children but wasn't around much for them.

Throughout the early 1960s, Haggard played guitar in small clubs in Bakersfield and Las Vegas, Nevada. He also recorded singles for a tiny label run by his manager, Fuzzy Owen. Big-time success came to Haggard when his version of Liz Anderson's song "(My Friends Are Gonna Be) Strangers" (1964) cracked the country Top 10. The hit led to a contract with Capitol Records.

Fiercely independent, Haggard combined folk, gospel, and jazz for a unique sound. He and his band, the Strangers, offered a tough alternative to Nashville. Songs such as "Workin' Man Blues" (1969) were based on personal experiences that working people could relate to.

Haggard met with controversy after the release of his 1969 hit "Okie from Muskogee." The hippie youth movement was in full flower at the time. The movement promoted peace, love, and sexual freedom. Throughout the United States, many young Americans were calling for racial equality. They also wanted the U.S. military to pull out of the war in Vietnam (1959–1975).

Haggard's song seemed to criticize the youth movement. He boasted of not burning a draft card—a gesture that was popular among young men who opposed the Vietnam War. (The U.S. government sent draft cards directing young men to serve in the armed forces.) The unapologetic Haggard was seen as the nation's number one hippie hater. Haggard later said that the song was meant to be a funny comment on small-town life. (Muskogee is a small town in Oklahoma.)

It took Haggard years to live down the "Okie from Muskogee" controversy. Like Johnny Cash, he also had to deal with a slump in his career and overcome substance abuse. But late in his career, he found success again. He received the 2010 Kennedy Center Honors, a famous award for accomplishment in the performing arts. And he released albums such as **Working in Tennessee** (2011). ★

Must Download Playlist

KITTY WELLS,
"It Wasn't God Who Made Honky-Tonk Angels" (1952)

JOHNNY CASH,
"I Walk the Line" (1956)

PATSY CLINE,
"I Fall to Pieces" (1961)

MERLE HAGGARD,
"Sing Me Back Home" (1967)

BUCK OWENS,
"Who's Gonna Mow Your Grass" (1969)

CONWAY TWITTY,
"Hello Darlin'" (1970)

CHARLIE RICH,
"Behind Closed Doors" (1973)

DOLLY PARTON,
"Jolene" (1973)

GEORGE JONES AND TAMMY WYNETTE,
"(We're Not) The Jet Set" (1974)

LORETTA LYNN,
"Portland Oregon" (2004)

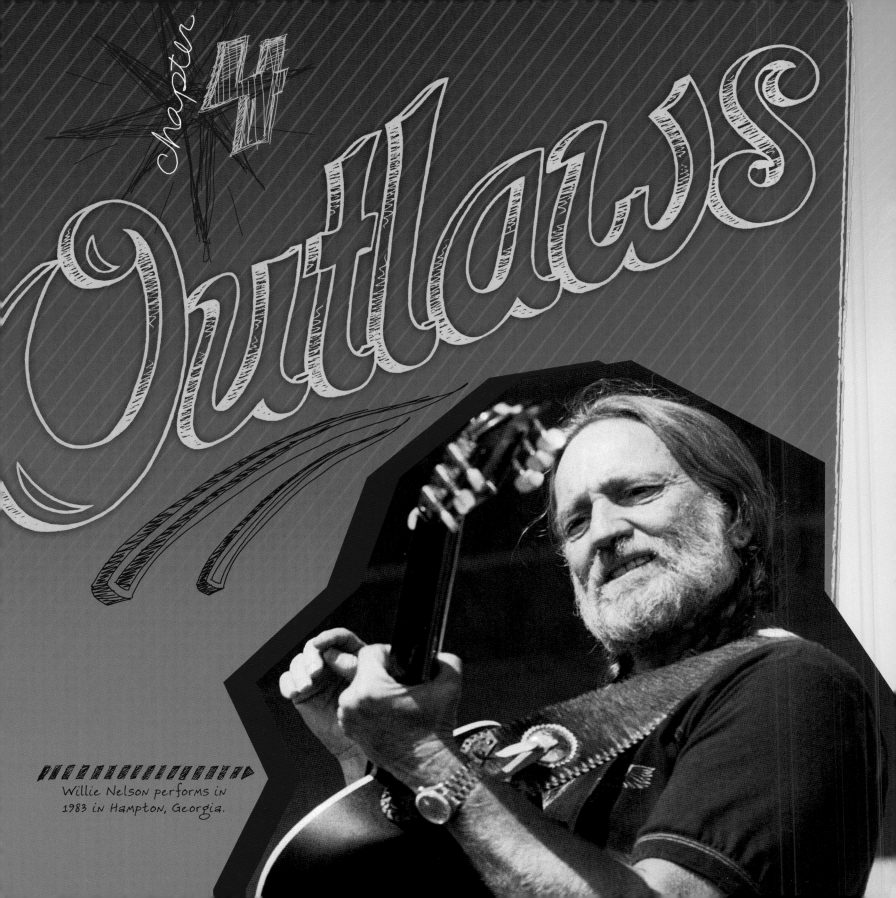

chapter 4

Outlaws

LONG BEFORE HE BECAME A PIGTAILED, FIT-FOR-MOUNT RUSHMORE COUNTRY LEGEND, WILLIE NELSON WAS AN ORDINARY GUY IN A TURTLENECK.

He was born in Texas in 1933 and worked as a Nashville songwriter. He made his living fashioning hits for other singers. One of his greatest includes "Crazy" (1961), which he wrote for Patsy Cline.

Nelson didn't have much success as a singer at first. His desire to record concept albums about difficult ideas was not popular. (Concept albums feature songs that share a common theme or that tell a single story.) Nelson wound up "in a bad odor with the Nashville establishment," said famed producer Jerry Wexler. For example, **Yesterday's Wine** (1971) was a thoughtful album with songs about death. The album "scared a lot of people," said Nelson. "[The record company] RCA's reaction was 'Who's gonna play this?'"

Following the failure of **Yesterday's Wine**, Nelson briefly retired from music. But he soon restarted his career in Texas. Hippies and college students in the capital city of Austin loved him.

Nelson formed his own family of musicians. They included his sister Bobbie Nelson on keyboards. In 1973 he began his annual Willie Nelson Fourth of July Picnic at Austin's Armadillo World Headquarters music hall. Nelson wanted this picnic to combine country music with the positive vibes of the Woodstock Music and Art Fair. A landmark music festival, Woodstock had taken place in New York in 1969.

In its first year, Nelson's festival was not well organized. Fighting between hippies and other groups was a problem. However, Nelson continued to arrange the festival in the years that followed. With time, he turned the picnic into the largest country music festival ever held.

WILLIE BRANCHES OUT

Willie Nelson moved across many styles in the 1970s. With **Shotgun Willie** (1973), he tried another concept album. The hard-edged record featured songs with themes of danger and rebellion. Nelson's next album was **Phases and Stages** (1974). It told of a married couple's rise and

The first Willie Nelson Fourth of July Picnic was in 1973. Nelson hosts this festival each year in Austin, Texas.

fall, from the husband's point of view and then the wife's. **Red Headed Stranger** in 1975 was a song series about an outlaw on the run. It later became a 1986 feature film starring Nelson.

In 1978 Nelson recorded **Stardust**, an album of popular standards and jazz classics. **Stardust** had people in the industry scratching their heads—until it became a best seller. The album stayed on the Billboard country charts for more than ten years. Its songs showcased Nelson's simple vocals and his jazzy guitar playing. **Stardust** inspired other country and pop artists such as Sting and Merle Haggard to record standards albums too.

THEN CAME WAYLON

The leathery-voiced singer Waylon Jennings joined Willie Nelson on the outlaw trail. Jennings had played guitar for early rocker Buddy Holly. He was a proud son of Lubbock, Texas. He moved to Nashville in 1965.

At first Jennings was a successful studio guitarist. He then established himself as a singer and songwriter. But like Nelson, he wanted more artistic freedom than was possible in Nashville. So he moved to Austin.

While in Texas, Jennings turned out hit albums such as **Honky Tonk Heroes** (1973). He also recorded the

COUNTRY LITE, '70S STYLE

A softer form of country gained popularity in the 1970s alongside outlaw music. The radio-friendly "Country Lite" was aimed at an easy-listening audience.

"Kiss an Angel Good Mornin,'" (1971) a million-selling recorded by **Charley Pride** (TOP) defined the Country Lite style. In 1993 Pride became the first African American inducted into the Grand Ole Opry.

Country Lite appealed to many pop artists. "I Honestly Love You," sung by Australian singer **Olivia Newton-John** (BOTTOM), was a huge country and pop hit in 1974. **Kenny Rogers** topped the country charts in 1977 with the collection Ten Years of Gold. That album featured country-style recordings of songs Rogers had recorded in the sixties with his rock-oriented group **First Edition**.

mega-selling "Are You Ready for the Country?" (1976) and other hit singles. As duet partners, Jennings and Nelson scored big with the singles "Mammas Don't Let Your Babies Grow Up to Be Cowboys" (1975) and "Luckenbach, Texas (Back to the Basics of Love)" (1977). In 1978 they recorded the album **Waylon & Willie**. They sang together again in the Highwaymen.

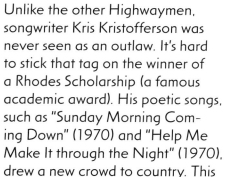

Waylon Jennings performs in 1984.

Kris Kristofferson and Rita Coolidge duet in 1971. Kristofferson became known for his poetic songwriting.

A POET, A PICKER, AND A MOVIE STAR

Unlike the other Highwaymen, songwriter Kris Kristofferson was never seen as an outlaw. It's hard to stick that tag on the winner of a Rhodes Scholarship (a famous academic award). His poetic songs, such as "Sunday Morning Coming Down" (1970) and "Help Me Make It through the Night" (1970), drew a new crowd to country. This crowd included fans of rock goddess Janis Joplin. Joplin's recording of Kristofferson's "Me and Bobby McGee" became a hit in 1971, a year after her death from a drug overdose. Kristofferson's starring role with singer Barbra Streisand in the film A Star Is Born (1976) didn't hurt the country cause, either.

Like Willie Nelson, Kristofferson has a unique, craggy voice. But many fans prefer Kristofferson's versions of his songs over smoother versions by other artists. Through much of the 1970s, Kristofferson performed with his then-wife Rita Coolidge. Coolidge started her career as a backup singer for rock singer Joe Cocker.

COUNTRY GOES ROCK

Country and rock 'n' roll first met through the rockabilly artists of the 1950s. In the sixties and the seventies, musicians hopped between the styles again. They created country rock. Many of the form's masterpieces came from Florida native

Gram Parsons. Parsons sparked new interest in classic country among rock fans. He had a gift for mixing rock with the sounds of country artists such as Buck Owens. He also put the sounds of gospel and soul into his yearning melodies.

With the rock group the Byrds, Parsons recorded the pioneering country-rock album **Sweetheart of the Rodeo** (1968). He then helped form a country rock band called the Flying Burrito Brothers. Parsons recorded the albums **GP** (1973) and **Grievous Angel** (1974) under his own name before dying in 1973 of a drug overdose.

Two unlikely heroes of country

rock gained fame as teen idols. From 1952 to 1966, Ricky Nelson starred in the TV sitcom The Adventures of Ozzie and Harriet. He also recorded a string of rockabilly hits including "Be-Bop Baby" (1957) and "Poor Little Fool" (1958). His rebirth as a country rock artist in the late sixties did not go over well with many fans. At a concert in 1970, some people booed Nelson when he refused to play his old hits. Nelson vented about this in his hit song "Garden Party" (1972).

Michael Nesmith became a star as a spaced-out member of the Monkees. The Monkees were a band and the stars of a 1960s TV comedy series. With the help of the best studio players and songwriters

Gram Parsons RIGHT ignored the line between country music and rock 'n' roll. Parsons and Ricky Nelson BOTTOM both recorded classic country-rock songs.

money could buy, the Monkees turned out hit after hit. Nesmith wrote some of them. He didn't have the same success when he formed a country rock group called the First National Band in 1969. But critics praised the group's recordings. The songs featured the great O. J. "Red" Rhodes on pedal steel guitar.

A DIFFERENT KIND OF REBEL

The outlaw movement wasn't the only alternative to mainstream country. In the 1980s, Rosanne Cash and her husband recorded a unique blend of country, pop, and folk music.

Cash was raised in Los Angeles by her mother, Vivian Liberto. Liberto had divorced Rosanne's father, Johnny Cash, in 1966. Rosanne grew up loving the Beatles, singer-songwriters Joni Mitchell and Jackson Browne, and Ray Charles's album **Modern Sounds in Country and Western Music** (1962). She moved to Nashville after high school to sing backup for her father. Rosanne later scored eleven number one country hits. Her breakthrough album was **Seven Year Ache** (1981). The album mixed original cuts such as the title song with covers of tunes such as Tom Petty's "Hometown Blues."

When **Rosanne Cash** (ABOVE) was eighteen, she loved pop, folk, and R & B. Some of her favorites were the **Beatles**, **Joni Mitchell**, and **Ray Charles**. But she wasn't listening to country music. So her father, **Johnny Cash**, put together a list of one hundred essential country songs. He gave Rosanne one of the greatest homework assignments ever: learn them. Over time she did that and more. For her 2009 album, **The List**, she recorded a dozen of those timeless tunes. The album's tracks include **Jimmie Rodgers's** "Miss the Mississippi and You" (1932) and **Hank Williams's** "Take These Chains from My Heart" (1953).

Cash refused to play by music industry rules, which included spending months on the road, promoting her records. This left her feeling isolated in Nashville. In 1991 she moved to New York, where she recorded her acclaimed album **The Wheel** (1993). Cash continued going her own way with **Rules of Travel** (2003). This album includes a heart-breaking duet, "September When It Comes," with her ailing father. Her 2006 album **Black Cadillac** features moving songs about coming to terms with the deaths of her father, mother, and stepmother.

RODNEY'S WINDING HIGHWAY

Well before singer, songwriter, and guitarist Rodney Crowell married Rosanne Cash, he was a kid in Houston, Texas. He loved listening to the music of Johnny Cash and Roy Acuff, as well as to Appalachian folk songs.

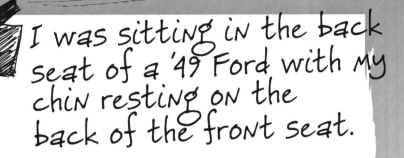

" I was sitting in the back seat of a '49 Ford with my chin resting on the back of the front seat.

We had this big chrome dashboard radio, but whatever was coming out of it wasn't reaching me.

Suddenly, [Johnny Cash's] 'I Walk the Line' came on and it hit me.... Hearing 'I Walk the Line' showed me what I wanted to do. "

—Rodney Crowell, 2001

EMMYLOU

Few artists in contemporary country are as loved and respected as **Emmylou Harris**. Throughout her career, the angelically voiced Harris has worked with gifted artists ranging from **Gram Parsons** to **Linda Ronstadt** to **Neil Young**. With producer Brian Ahern, she released two classic albums in 1975—Pieces of the Sky and Elite Hotel. These records helped pave the way for other country singer-songwriters in the 1980s. And in recording the music of **Buck Owens** and **Hank Williams**, she stirred new interest in these country legends. Later on, Harris earned praise for her bold versions of rock and folk classics in the album Wrecking Ball (1995). She has also recorded more of her own songs on Stumble into Grace (2003).

Emmylou Harris performs in the 1970s. Harris has scored many solo hits. She has also partnered with artists such as Gram Parsons and Neil Young.

HIT-MAKING MOM and DAUGHTER

The Judds—mother **Naomi** (RIGHT) **and daughter Wynonna (born Christina Ciminella)** (LEFT)—dominated the 1980s with hits including "Why Not Me" (1984), "Grandpa (Tell Me 'Bout the Good Old Days)" (1986), and "Give a Little Love" (1988). When Naomi was diagnosed with liver problems in 1991, the duo's career ended. Wynonna decided to go it alone. Since then she's had some success on her own with albums such as *Wynonna* (1992) and *Sing: Chapter 1* (2009).

Crowell began his musical career in Nashville. In 1975 he was drafted as a singer and rhythm guitarist for singer Emmylou Harris. She recorded many of his songs, including "Leaving Louisiana in the Broad Daylight" (1978) and "'Til I Gain Control Again" (1981). As a result, Crowell's reputation grew. In the 1980s, he began collaborating with Rosanne Cash in Nashville.

Crowell's solo albums were acclaimed because of his soulful voice and rock 'n' roll energy. But they didn't sell many copies. After switching record labels and taking a break to produce Rosanne Cash, Crowell hit pay dirt with **Diamonds & Dirt** (1988). He scored five number one country hits with the album,

Rodney Crowell, pictured here in 2004, is known for soulful, rocking country albums such as **Diamonds & Dirt** (1988).

including the Grammy-winning "After All This Time." The follow-up album, **Keys to the Highway** (1989), produced two more big hits. Even so, Crowell's marriage to Cash ended in 1992, along with their creative partnership.

In 2001 Crowell pulled himself out of a rut with **The Houston Kid**. The record showed that he had only improved as an artist. Crowell continued to turn out thoughtful albums over the years, including **Fate's Right Hand** (2003). ★

MUST DOWNLOAD Playlist

BYRDS,
"One Hundred Years from Now" (1968)

FLYING BURRITO BROTHERS,
"Do Right Woman" (1969)

KRIS KRISTOFFERSON,
"Sunday Morning Coming Down" (1970)

CHARLEY PRIDE,
"Kiss an Angel Good Mornin'" (1971)

GRAM PARSONS WITH EMMYLOU HARRIS,
"Hearts on Fire" (1974)

WAYLON JENNINGS,
"Are You Ready for the Country" (1976)

WILLIE NELSON,
"Whiskey River" (1979)

ROSANNE CASH,
"Seven Year Ache" (1981)

JUDDS,
"Give a Little Love" (1988)

RODNEY CROWELL,
"Earthbound" (2003)

chapter 5

CROSSING OVER AND Crossing Back

Randy Travis sings at a tribute for musician John Lennon in 1990.

WHEN DWIGHT YOAKAM MOVED TO LOS ANGELES IN 1978, IT DIDN'T SEEM LIKE THE WISEST DECISION FOR AN ASPIRING COUNTRY SINGER.

At that time, punk and heavy-metal bands were all the rage. They played rock music that was fast, aggressive, and loud.

Yoakam had tried to make it in Nashville after dropping out of college. But his taste for honky-tonk, hillbilly music, and bluegrass was not popular there. The Urban Cowboy sound was lighting up the pop charts. Urban Cowboy artists such as Mickey Gilley and Johnny Lee recorded smooth, glossy country songs meant for listeners in cities.

So Yoakam went west. He related to the energy and swagger of the L.A. punk bands. With his lean looks and natural snarl, he struck a punkish pose himself. Performing on bills with the punk band X and the rootsy Blasters, he won fans by making honky-tonk sexy and mysterious. By the late 1980s, he was selling out arenas.

Working with producer-guitarist Pete Anderson, Yoakam scored nine Top 10 hits in the eighties, including "Streets of Bakersfield" (1988) with Buck Owens. Then came the smash 1993 album **This Time**. The release won Yoakam a Grammy for Best Male Country Vocal for "Ain't That Lonely Yet."

Yoakam was not the only choice outside of Urban Cowboy music in the 1980s. Major stars included hit-making honky-tonker George Strait and the deep-voiced traditionalist Randy Travis.

Buck Owens LEFT and Dwight Yoakam RIGHT hang out in front of a Cadillac in 1988.

Canada's k. d. lang LEFT made waves among country fans in the late 1980s.

Canadian singer k. d. lang also wowed fans. With her velvety voice, sense of humor, and androgynous (neither male nor female) look, lang was controversial at first. A huge fan of Patsy Cline, lang recorded the **Shadowland** album (1988) with Cline's famous producer Owen Bradley. This album shot her to stardom. She went on to record in many different musical styles.

IT'S GARTH TIME

Oklahoma boy Garth Brooks was a 1990s superstar who went places no country star had gone before. His rise inspired a *Forbes* magazine cover story called "Country Conquers Rock."

Brooks came to country music from 1970s rock music. He was a big fan of the hard rock of Kiss, the pop rock of Queen, and the working-class rock of Bruce Springsteen. Garth Brooks's concerts were

In the 1990s, Garth Brooks became an international sensation.

GARTH GETS ALL SHOOK UP

In 1999 the Recording Industry Association of America (RIAA) named Garth Brooks the best-selling solo artist in the United States. His 1991 album Ropin' the Wind was the first album to debut at number one on the pop and country charts. His 1992 follow-up, The Chase, repeated this feat. Brooks's 1994 collection, The Hits, was the biggest-selling greatest-hits album in country history.

The Elvis Presley estate and Presley's record label protested the RIAA's decision. The protest caused the RIAA to change the way it measured sales. For instance, the organization chose to give more weight to Presley's singles from the 1950s. (At that time, singles were a more common format than albums.) In 2006 Presley was returned to the number one spot.

The RIAA reversed itself in 2007 and restored Brooks at the top. In 2010 the RIAA reversed its position yet again and gave the title of best-selling solo artist to Presley. By 2012 Presley had sold 133.5 million records, according to the RIAA. Brooks had sold 128 million.

spectacles. He made his entrance in an elevator, with lights flashing and explosions sounding. He was also known to swing over audiences on a cable.

For all Brooks's flashiness, he came across as an ordinary, thoughtful guy. With his third album, **Ropin' the Wind** (1991), Brooks became the first country artist to enter the pop album charts at number one. Six of his albums earned diamond status (more than ten million copies sold). When his sales slowed, he introduced a rock-star alter ego on Garth Brooks in . . . The Life of Chris Gaines (1999). The stunt was meant to lead to a Hollywood movie in which Brooks would star as the character Chris Gaines. It flopped. The movie never got made.

In 2000 Brooks announced his retirement from music. He sometimes performs for charities and benefits. For example, Brooks raised money for victims of Hurricane Katrina in 2005 and victims of the Nashville flood of 2009.

ALT CURRENTS

In 1990 the Illinois band Uncle Tupelo released **No Depression**. The album introduced alternative country (alt-country, or Americana). Alt-country was like country rock. But it had a bolder attitude and was popular with more people. Alt-country acts such as Uncle Tupelo and Whiskeytown were influenced by punk rock and New Wave music of the 1970s and the 1980s. The music featured string instruments such as mandolins, fiddles, and banjos. It also had the punch of punk. Alt-country songs talked about the struggles of workers in the Midwest.

In 1993 Uncle Tupelo released its first major-label album, **Anodyne** (1993). But the band's leaders, Jay Farrar and Jeff Tweedy, couldn't resolve their differences. The band broke up soon afterward. Tweedy formed the band Wilco in Chicago. Wilco moved from country into adventurous pop music with **Yankee Hotel Foxtrot** (2002). It had mainstream success with **Wilco (The Album)** (2009) and **The Whole Love** (2011). Jay Farrar formed Son Volt in Saint Louis, Missouri. His band specializes in thoughtful songs with piercing guitar solos.

Other popular alt-country musicians include the African American string band the Carolina Chocolate Drops and the sweet-voiced folk-rock singer Tift Merritt. Flaco Jiménez is an alt-country accordion master. Hard-edged singer-songwriter Lucinda Williams is another alt-country musician.

Her powerful album **Blessed** was released in 2011.

ACHING, BREAKING, AND MORE HIT MAKING

The early to mid-1990s were an exciting time for country music. The music surged in popularity thanks to artists such as Garth Brooks. Billy Ray Cyrus's 1992 hit "Achy Breaky Heart" sold so many copies so quickly it became a defining hit of the decade. A classic one-hit wonder, Cyrus became better known as the father of pop sensation Miley Cyrus.

Oklahoma native Vince Gill was one of the most appealing country stars to come from Nashville in the 1990s. Gill is an ace guitarist with a voice of great warmth. He has recorded duets with country greats such as Dolly Parton and Rosanne Cash. And he has written many albums' worth of moving songs. In 2006 Gill showed off his musical range on the four-disc set **These Days**.

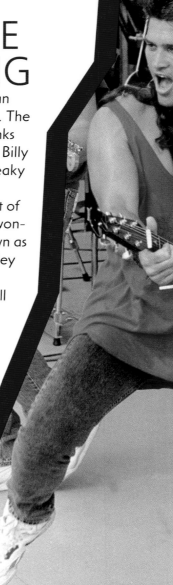

Billy Ray Cyrus served up one of the biggest hits of the 1990s, the pop-country tune "Achy Breaky Heart" (1992).

CONTROVERSY

Politics and country music sometimes don't mix. In 2003 the Dixie Chicks drew protests from some country fans. Natalie Maines told an audience at a concert in London, England, that the band was ashamed that U.S. president George W. Bush was from Texas. At that time, the United States was leading a war in Iraq that President Bush supported. Maines spoke out against this war. Many American fans believed Maines's comments were unpatriotic. They boycotted (refused to buy) the group's music. The Dixie Chicks went on to new success with releases such as *Taking the Long Way* (2006). This album won the 2007 Grammy Award for Album of the Year.

In the late 1990s, no country act created the excitement of the Dixie Chicks. This Texas trio combined spirited vocals, crowd-pleasing instrumental licks, and outspoken personalities. Early on, the Chicks changed their lineup a few times. With singer Natalie Maines and sisters Martie Maguire and Emily Robison on various instruments, the band's members became superstars. Their hit albums include **Wide Open Spaces** (1998) and **Fly** (1999).

CROSSOVER SENSATIONS

The Dixie Chicks and Garth Brooks were among many country stars with crossover success. Reba McEntire proved herself to be a multitalented artist too. She rose to country stardom in the 1980s with albums such as **My Kind of Country** (1984), a collection of her favorite songs. In the 1990s, she acted in films such as the creepy comedy Tremors (1990). In the early 2000s, she

Emily Robison LEFT, Natalie Maines MIDDLE, and Martie Maguire RIGHT of the Dixie Chicks perform at the Grammy Awards in 2003.

starred in her own TV sitcom, *Reba*. She also appeared in Broadway musicals such as *Annie Get Your Gun* and *South Pacific*.

Mississippi native Faith Hill was another major crossover star. Her streak of southern soul set her apart. Hill's first single, "Wild One" (1994), spent four weeks atop the *Billboard* charts. She was the first female country singer to have such a successful debut since the 1960s.

Hill's 1998 single "This Kiss" and her 1999 album **Breathe** had a pop feel, and Hill conquered the mainstream market. However, songs from her pop-inspired 2002 album **Cry** failed to crack country's Top 10. So Hill went back to a more traditional country sound. Her 2006 Soul-2Soul II Tour with her husband, singer Tim McGraw, was the highest-earning country music tour of all time.

Country's greatest female crossover star was Canadian Shania Twain. Twain's producer, Mutt Lange, was known for his work with hard-rock groups AC/DC and Def Leppard. Beginning with the 1995 album **The Woman in Me**, Lange filled Twain's albums with arena-ready pop hooks. With albums such as **Come on Over** (1997), Twain became the top-selling female country singer of all time. She also married Lange.

In 2009 Twain was a guest judge and mentor on TV's *American Idol*. Before her trip to *Idol*, Twain had spent several years out of the public eye. Her marriage to Lange ended, and she lost the ability to sing for a time. Twain detailed these chapters in her private life on her Oprah-channel reality series, *Why Not? with Shania Twain*, and in a 2011 memoir, *From This Moment On*.

Shania Twain rocks the Country Music Awards in 2002. Hits such as "That Don't Impress Me Much" (1997) won Twain a huge following among both country and pop fans.

BACK TO THE MOUNTAINS

O Brother, Where Art Thou? was a 2000 film by Joel Coen and Ethan Coen. The movie was set during the 1930s in the American South. Its sound track boasted new roots music. Roots music celebrates the bluegrass and mountain music of old. Legendary producer Joseph "T Bone" Burnett supervised the recordings. Artists included Tennessee gospel legends the Fairfield Four, Louisiana bluegrass group the Cox Family, and Emmylou Harris. The sound track's music sounded

ANOTHER KIND OF CROSSOVER

It's not unusual for rock musicians to go country. In fact, on his 1994 hit "Gone Country," soft-spoken country star Alan Jackson pokes fun at faded rockers who go to Nashville to revive their careers. For example, Bret Michaels of the rock band Poison sang a duet with Kenny Chesney. Rock megastar Jon Bon Jovi and Sugarland's Jennifer Nettles had a number one country hit with "Who Says You Can't Go Home?" (2006).

Darius Rucker (TOP) made the switch to country so successfully there's a good chance some fans have never heard of his earlier band. Rucker is the former lead singer of the rock band Hootie & the Blowfish. In 1994 Hootie had a massive-selling album, Cracked Rear View. In 2008 Rucker saw his first single, "Don't Think I Don't Know about It," soar to number one on the Hot Country Songs charts. Rucker became the first African American to be named best new artist by the Country Music Association. He followed his first hit with four more chart-toppers.

Detroit rap-rocker Kid Rock (Bob Ritchie) (BOTTOM) hasn't abandoned the music that made him a star. But he has also been successful as a country crossover act. He had his first country hit in 2008 with the Southern-rock song "All Summer Long." He later recorded a duet with Martina McBride, the 2011 song "Care." Kid Rock also charmed country fans as host of the 2010 and 2011 CMT Music Awards.

T Bone Burnett put together the surprise-smash sound track to the film **O Brother, Where Art Thou?** (2000).

THE ROOTS REVIVAL CONTINUES

T Bone Burnett failed to match the success of **O Brother** with his sound track for the Civil War romance *Cold Mountain* (2003). But that didn't mean Americans' love affair with roots music was over. In 2007 Burnett produced **Raising Sand**, a collaboration between country singer-fiddler Alison Krauss and rocker Robert Plant. The singers duetted on an assortment of rock, blues, and country covers. Their album won five awards at the 2009 Grammys, including Album of the Year.

Raising Sand was as surprising a success as **O Brother**. Krauss is a bluegrass fiddler from Champaign, Illinois, with a lovely, pure-toned voice. She had had earlier success among country fans as a member of the group Union Station. Plant was the wailing, lion-maned former singer for British metal band Led Zeppelin. But the duo harmonized as if they had been doing it their whole life.

a lot like old-time country music. For that reason, radio stations and CMT did not play it. Even so, the sound track sold millions of copies. *O Brother's* music also cleaned up at the 2001 Grammys, winning awards including Album of the Year.

Those looking to understand this unlikely success need look no further than September 11, 2001. Sales of the **O Brother** sound track took off months after its December 2000 release. The music served as a kind of musical comfort food in the aftermath of the 9/11 terrorist attacks in New York and near Washington, D.C. Its timeless mountain folk and bluegrass sounds carried listeners away from the troubles of the modern world. By June 2011, the **O Brother** album had sold more than seven million copies.

Alison Krauss LEFT and Robert Plant RIGHT perform a song from their award-winning album **Raising Sand** (2007).

FROM CHARLEY PRIDE to the CAROLINA CHOCOLATE DROPS

More than thirty years after being signed by RCA Records, the semiretired singer Charley Pride remains one of country music's only African American stars. When Darius Rucker topped the Hot Country Songs chart in 2008 with "Don't Think I Don't Think about It," he became the first African American to do so since Pride in 1983. And Rucker became the first African American to be named best new artist by the Country Music Association.

Many black artists have made inroads into country music. One of the first was the black hillbilly star DeFord Bailey in the 1920s. Ray Charles's Modern Sounds in Country and Western Music (1962) is a classic of both country and R & B. And in 1993, Aaron Neville won a Grammy Award for his recording of George Jones's "The Grand Tour." More recently, pop singer Lionel Ritchie recorded songs with country stars such as Jason Aldean, Tim McGraw, and Rascal Flatts on his hit album Tuskegee (2012).

Even so, many factors have limited African American opportunities in country music. Country music is marketed (advertised) to a largely white audience. And some people associate country with prejudiced racial attitudes of the past.

The good news is that groups such as the black string band the Carolina Chocolate Drops have become crowd favorites. The Grammy-winning Carolina Chocolate Drops (ABOVE) have also hit No. 1 on the U.S. bluegrass charts with albums such as Leaving Eden (2012). Other African American artists such as Louisiana's Trini Triggs are on the verge of widespread success. When rapper Lil Wayne can perform at the Country Music Awards, which he did with Kid Rock in 2008, change is afoot.

Gillian Welch, pictured here in 2007, found fame with her raw, personal approach to country music.

Welch and Rawlings are artists of high standards. They went eight years between the album **Soul Journey** (2003) and the 2011 record **The Harrow and the Harvest**. Some critics have attacked Welch for performing in a style that doesn't reflect her life experience. She has stood up to the criticism with mesmerizing tales of poverty, drug addiction, and religious struggle.

SOUL JOURNEYING

Gillian Welch was another talented contributor to **O Brother**. Welch grew up in California, the adopted daughter of television composers. She started out playing moody rock music. She became obsessed with Appalachian music—especially the songs of the Carter Family and the Stanley Brothers. After attending college in Boston, Welch settled in Nashville. She formed a roots music duo with guitarist David Rawlings. Their first album, **Revival**, arrived in 1996.

NEW MILLENNIUM BLUEGRASS

Traditional bluegrass doesn't have much in common with hip-hop or dubstep. Bluegrass features clean arrangements, high harmonizing vocals, and no drums. But a new generation of string bands is playing bluegrass for young listeners. These bands have fun names such as the Duhks and the Mammals. The groups have updated the old-time music from the twenties and the thirties that led to bluegrass.

"Old-time and rock 'n' roll are not that different," said Mammals guitarist Tao Rodriguez-Seeger. "When you play these old instruments with a [wild] attitude, it's like a driving punk band."

The biggest star to emerge from the bluegrass revival is hot-wired mandolinist Chris Thile. Thile first made a name as a member of Nickel Creek. Nickel Creek began as an acoustic bluegrass trio and became a popular crossover band. Thile's new band, the Punch Brothers, takes bluegrass places it has never been. Punch Brothers songs mix old-time music with jazz and progressive rock. Their 2012 album, **Who's Feeling Young Now?**, includes a version of the rock band Radiohead's "Kid A."

 Now you can play a banjo in front of teenagers and not have them make fun of you.

—Ruth Ungar of the Mammals on the bluegrass revival, 2006

TAYLORING COUNTRY

Modern country music can be anything it wants to be. Divisions between country and pop no longer mean anything to artists and their fans. One example is Taylor

Taylor Swift sings for the crowd in Perth, Australia, in 2012. Swift is the latest country musician to become a global star.

Swift. Her dominance of country music charts and award shows has been phenomenal.

Swift's self-titled 2006 album made it clear that she had a gift for pop melodies. But that album didn't prepare listeners for her confident 2008 album, **Fearless**. The release was the best-selling album of 2008 and 2009. On **Fearless**, Swift spoke to and for average teens. Fans related to the wallflower longings of "You Belong with Me." Swift put

hard-earned teen wisdom into "Fifteen." Then came the album **Speak Now** (2010). In the songs on this album, Swift sang honestly about relationships that went bust. Like singer-songwriters of the sixties, she wasn't shy about calling out people who had mistreated her.

Swift has faced a backlash since becoming a country sensation. In a bizarre moment during the 2009 MTV Video Music Awards, hip-hop star Kanye West interrupted Swift's Best Female Video acceptance speech. He argued that R & B singer Beyoncé should have won the award. Some critics question Swift's vocal talent. For example, she sounded off-key in a duet with singer Stevie Nicks during the 2010 Grammy Awards. But Swift has shown that superstardom is the best revenge. She sells out arenas and continues to receive many awards and nominations.

KENNY AND BRAD

Kenny Chesney and Brad Paisley have both drawn fans to arenas while carving out their own distinctive musical styles. With his sleeveless shirts and laid-back attitude, Chesney is country's easygoing champion. In most of his songs, he seeks sun, fun, and cool drinks. The

The music of Brad Paisley, performing here in 2010, gives traditional country themes a clever spin.

wanting a car as a kid and a long day of fishing. He always puts a funny, clever spin on such tunes. Paisley also lights up his songs with dazzling guitar playing. When he does get serious, he isn't afraid to tackle subjects that many other singers avoid. For example, some Republican fans did not like Paisley's song "Welcome to the Future" (2009). In this song, Paisley expresses his awe over the 2008 election of Democrat Barack Obama as the nation's first African American president. But Paisley balances that song with tunes such as "This Is Country Music" (2010), which celebrates country's traditional values.

COUNTRY LOOKS FORWARD

There is no lack of sparkle in country's future. In 2009 Lady Antebellum became unstoppable with the trio's monster hit "Need You Now" and the album of the same name. This trio owes even more to pop music than Taylor Swift. The trio also boasts seamless vocal harmonies and moving love songs. After multiple wins at the 2011 Grammy Awards, Lady Antebellum took home the 2012 Best Country Album Grammy for **Own the Night**.

Chesney hit "No Shoes, No Shirt, No Problems" (2002) is just one example.

Chesney was born in Knoxville, Tennessee. He moved to Nashville in 1991. He moved slowly but surely toward success, crafting melodic hooks that were made to sing along with. Chesney has shown that he is deepening as an artist with the 2010 album **Hemingway's Whiskey**. Duets with the great George Jones and the young rocker Grace Potter reveal Chesney's wide range.

Brad Paisley has written songs about down-home topics such as

Blake Shelton LEFT and Miranda Lambert RIGHT sing a duet at the Academy of Country Music Fan Jam in 2011.

Along with the Band Perry and Sugarland, Lady Antebellum has made boy-girl country bands a force in country music.

Miranda Lambert is another new talent. She began her career with a series of nail-tough releases and became one of country's leading artists. In 2011 she released two very different albums. **Four the Record** includes a duet with her smooth-singing husband, Blake Shelton (a judge on TV's The Voice). The album's styles range from alt-country to pop balladry. On **Hell on Heels**, Lambert sings in a classic country fashion. She recorded this album as a member of the all-female trio Pistol Annies.

And country still has its share of hard-living male artists. Streetwise singer Eric Church broke through with his 2011 gem **Chief**. Trace Adkins is a hit maker and a self-described "freethinking roughneck." But all these years after Jimmie Rodgers fathered modern country, the music is still defining itself. Country continues to branch out and convert new listeners. American Idol winners—and country singers—Scotty McCreery and Lauren Alaina in 2011 prove that America is always ready for more country. ★

MUST DOWNLOAD Playlist

UNCLE TUPELO,
"The Long Cut" (1993)

DWIGHT YOAKAM,
"A Thousand Miles from Nowhere" (1993)

STEVE EARLE,
"More Than I Can Do" (1996)

WHISKEYTOWN,
"Excuse Me While I Break My Own Heart Tonight" (1997)

LUCINDA WILLIAMS,
"2 Kool 2 Be 4-Gotten" (1998)

MIRANDA LAMBERT,
"Kerosene" (2005)

GARTH BROOKS,
"More Than a Memory" (2007)

ALISON KRAUSS AND ROBERT PLANT,
"Gone, Gone, Gone (Done Moved On)" (2007)

TAYLOR SWIFT,
"You Belong with Me" (2008)

BRAD PAISLEY,
"Welcome to the Future" (2009)

OLD 97'S,
"Perfume" (2011)

GLOSSARY

alt-country: a style of country music known for its mixture of traditional country sounds, punk rock, and folk music. Alt-country is also known as alternative country and Americana.

ballad: a song that tells a story with its lyrics. Ballads are often slow, romantic, or mournful.

bluegrass: a style of country music that features high-pitched singing and fast playing of instruments. Bluegrass is usually played with string instruments, including fiddle, banjo, guitar, mandolin, and bass.

blues: a form of African American folk music. Blues lyrics are often sorrowful but sometimes uplifting.

country rock: a style of music that blends traditional country music with elements of rock 'n' roll

crossover: to be popular in different musical genres or with many different types of listeners

hillbilly music: an early style of country music performed in the southeastern United States beginning in the 1920s. Hillbilly music has its roots in the folk music of England, Ireland, and Scotland.

honky-tonk: a rowdy style of country music performed in working-class bars in Texas beginning in the late 1930s

Nashville sound: a style of country music created in Nashville, Tennessee, in the 1950s. Songs with the Nashville sound often featured strings and soothing background vocals. This music was meant to appeal to listeners who did not like rough rockabilly music.

old-time music: a group of country music styles from the 1920s and the 1930s. The old-time sound features string bands and groups singing in harmony.

outlaw country: a movement in country music of the 1970s. Outlaw singers and songwriters wrote songs about their personal lives. They also brought rock music's themes of independence and rebellion to country music.

rockabilly: a style of music that mixes rock 'n' roll and hillbilly music as well as blues and R & B. Rockabilly songs often have driving rhythms and themes of danger or social unrest.

roots music: modern country music that borrows from hillbilly music, bluegrass, and other earlier styles of country music

string band: a musical group with instruments such as acoustic guitars, fiddles, banjos, and mandolins

Western swing: a danceable style of country music that was strongly influenced by jazz music of the 1930s and the 1940s

TIMELINE

1927: Jimmie Rodgers and the Carter Family make their first recordings for famed record scout Ralph Peer. Meanwhile, the Nashville radio station WSM's *Barn Dance* program officially becomes *The Grand Ole Opry*.

1934: Bob Wills forms the soon-to-be-legendary Western swing band the Texas Playboys.

1935: Patsy Montana becomes the first female country artist to sell a million records with "I Want to Be a Cowboy's Sweetheart."

1938: Singer Roy Acuff joins the cast of *The Grand Ole Opry*. The following year, he records the song "Great Speckled Bird."

1942: Roy Acuff teams with songwriter Fred Rose to form the music publishing company Acuff-Rose in Nashville, Tennessee. The center of the country music business soon shifts to Nashville.

1947: Two years after Earl Scruggs and Lester Flatt join Bill Monroe's Blue Grass Boys, the band records the iconic song "Blue Moon of Kentucky."

1953: Only four years after scoring his first number one country hit, "Lovesick Blues," Hank Williams dies in the backseat of his Cadillac on New Year's Day.

1954: Elvis Presley bursts on the scene with the two-sided single "That's All Right" and "Blue Moon of Kentucky."

1961: Patsy Cline releases two of her greatest hits, "Crazy" and "I Fall to Pieces." Two years later, she dies in a plane crash. Meanwhile, the Country Music Hall of Fame inducts its first members, Jimmie Rodgers, Fred Rose, and Hank Williams.

1967: Charley Pride becomes the first African American to perform at the *Grand Ole Opry* since harmonica player DeFord Bailey, a regular from 1925 to 1941.

1970: *The Johnny Cash Show* has its first season on ABC-TV.

1973: Patsy Cline becomes the first female solo artist to be inducted into the Country Music Hall of Fame.

1976: *Wanted! The Outlaws*, featuring Willie Nelson, Waylon Jennings, Jessi Colter, and Tompall Glaser, becomes country's first platinum album (more than one million copies sold) and the outlaw movement's biggest success.

1983: Country Music Television (CMT), the first cable television network devoted to country music, premieres.

1989: Garth Brooks scores his first big hit, "If Tomorrow Never Comes."

1997: Shania Twain releases the smash crossover album *Come on Over*. One year later, Faith Hill puts out another crossover hit, *Faith*.

2001: The best-selling, Grammy-winning sound track to the film *O Brother, Where Art Thou?* triggers a nationwide interest in old-time mountain music.

2003: Dixie Chicks singer Natalie Maines criticizes President George W. Bush at a concert in London, England.

2012: Garth Brooks is inducted into the Country Music Hall of Fame.

MINI BIOS

Roy Acuff (1903–1992): Tennessee native Roy Acuff was the first singing star of *The Grand Ole Opry*. He earned the name the King of Country. In 1942 Acuff and songwriter Fred Rose formed country music's first publishing house, Acuff-Rose Publications.

The Carter Family (A. P., 1891–1960; Maybelle, 1909–1978; Sara, 1898–1979): The Carters emerged from southwestern Virginia in the 1920s. Their gospel-tinged songs have never gone out of fashion. The songwriter A.P. sang in a striking low voice, while Maybelle played a guitar and Sara played guitar and autoharp.

Johnny Cash (1932–2003): Arkansas native Johnny Cash was one of the largest figures in country. He put a stamp on the music with songs such as "I Walk the Line" (1956), hosted a prime-time TV show, and reclaimed stardom late in life after a career downturn.

Patsy Cline (1932–1963): A native of Virginia, Cline is one of country's most beloved singers. She died in a plane crash after recording two of country's greatest ballads, "I Fall to Pieces" (1961) and "Crazy" (1961). In 1985 Cline was immortalized in the biographical Hollywood film *Sweet Dreams*, starring Jessica Lange.

Waylon Jennings (1937–2002): Texas singer-songwriter Waylon Jennings was Willie Nelson's comrade in the outlaw country movement. He scored hits with songs such as "Are You Ready for the Country" (1976). He often worked with his wife, singer Jessi Colter.

George Jones (born 1931): The Texas original George Jones is considered by many to be the greatest singer country has ever known. Jones took part in both the honky-tonk and Nashville sound movements. He also mastered the duet form with his wife, Tammy Wynette.

Willie Nelson (born 1933): Willie Nelson was a leading Nashville songwriter in the 1960s. In the decade that followed, Nelson moved back to his native Texas and became the leader of country's outlaw movement. He also established the successful country music festival Willie Nelson's Fourth of July Picnic, which is held every year in Austin.

Buck Owens (1929–2006): Buck Owens shook up Nashville in the early 1960s, scoring hit after hit with his California crew, the Buckaroos. His rebellious reputation suffered when, in 1969, he began hosting the country TV variety show *Hee Haw*. However, he deeply influenced later country musicians, including Dwight Yoakam.

Dolly Parton (born 1946): Born in Sevier County, Tennessee, Dolly Parton wrote and sang some of the deepest country songs of the late 1960s and the early 1970s. She also enjoyed success on the pop charts and in films such as *9 to 5* (1980) and *Steel Magnolias* (1989). In 1986 Parton took on a new role as the owner of her amusement park Dollywood.

Charley Pride (born 1938): Born in Sledge, Mississippi, the pioneering black country artist Charley Pride won over fans with hits such as "Just Between You and Me" (1967) and "Kiss an Angel Good Mornin'" (1971). Pride became the first African American member of the *Grand Ole Opry* in 1993.

Jimmie Rodgers (1897–1933): The Father of Country, Jimmie Rodgers, died young, his career cut short by tuberculosis. During his brief lifetime, Rodgers revolutionized music with his Blue Yodels series and other songs. His music drew upon his experience working on railroad lines as a young man in Mississippi.

Hank Williams (1923–1953): Alabama native Hank Williams overcame a difficult upbringing to change the face of country music. Numerous artists have covered Williams songs such as "Your Cheatin' Heart" (1952). He died young, passing away at the age of twenty-nine from a combination of health problems and alcohol abuse.

COUNTRY MUST-HAVES

Must-Have Albums

Buck Owens, *Buck Owens Sings Harlan Howard* (1961)

Ray Charles, *Modern Sounds in Country and Western Music* (1962)

Johnny Cash, *At Folsom Prison* (1968)

Byrds, *Sweetheart of the Rodeo* (1968)

Merle Haggard, *Same Train, A Different Time: Songs of Jimmie Rodgers* (1969)

Dolly Parton, *Coat of Many Colors* (1971)

Waylon Jennings, *Honky Tonk Heroes* (1973)

Willie Nelson, *Red Headed Stranger* (1975)

George Jones, *I Am What I Am* (1980)

Steve Earle, *Guitar Town* (1986)

Randy Travis, *Always & Forever* (1987)

Garth Brooks, *No Fences* (1990)

Dwight Yoakam, *This Time* (1993)

Emmylou Harris, *Wrecking Ball* (1995)

Whiskeytown, *Strangers Almanac* (1997)

Lucinda Williams, *Car Wheels on a Gravel Road* (1998)

Various Artists, *O Brother, Where Art Thou?* (2000)

Gillian Welch, *Time (The Revelator)* (2001)

Loretta Lynn, *Van Lear Rose* (2004)

Vince Gill, *These Days* (2006)

Miranda Lambert, *Crazy Ex-Girlfriend* (2007)

Jamie Johnson, *That Lonesome Song* (2008)

Darius Rucker, *Learn to Live* (2008)

Elizabeth Cook, *Welder* (2010)

Taylor Swift, *Speak Now* (2010)

Brad Paisley, *This Is Country Music* (2011)

Must-Have Songs

Bill Monroe and His Blue Grass Boys, "Blue Moon of Kentucky" (1947)

Bob Wills and His Texas Playboys, "Faded Love" (1950)

Hank Williams, "Your Cheatin' Heart" (1953)

Louvin Brothers, "When I Stop Dreaming" (1955)

Johnny Horton, "Battle of New Orleans" (1959)

Lefty Frizzell, "Long Black Veil" (1959)

Patsy Cline, "Crazy" (1961)

Ernest Tubb, "Waltz Across Texas" (1965)

Ray Price, "For the Good Times" (1970)

Dolly Parton, "Coat of Many Colors" (1971)

Charley Pride, "Kiss an Angel Good Mornin'" (1971)

Sammi Smith, "Help Me Make It through the Night" (1971)

Billy Swan, "I Can Help" (1974)

Gram Parsons and Emmylou Harris, "Love Hurts" (1974)

Freddy Fender, "Before the Next Teardrop Falls" (1975)

David Allen Coe, "You Never Even Called Me by My Name" (1975)

Johnny Paycheck, "Take This Job and Shove It" (1977)

Willie Nelson and Merle Haggard, "Poncho and Lefty" (1983)

Randy Travis, "On the Other Hand" (1985)

George Strait, "All My Ex's Live in Texas" (1987)

Dwight Yoakam, "A Thousand Miles from Nowhere" (1993)

LeAnn Rimes, "Blue" (1996)

Flatlanders, "Julia" (2002)

Buddy Miller, "With God on Our Side" (2004)

Lady Antebellum, "Need You Now" (2009)

Josh Turner, "All Over Me" (2010)

Eric Church, "Springsteen" (2012)

MAJOR AWARDS

Academy of Country Music (ACM): The ACM was founded in Los Angeles, California, in 1964 to promote country music on the West Coast. The organization was originally named the Country and Western Music Academy. It hosts an award show each year. Winners of the 2011 ACMs were Miranda Lambert for Top Female Vocalist and Video of the Year, "The House That Built Me;" Taylor Swift for Entertainer of the Year; and Lady Antebellum for Best Album (*Need You Now*).

American Country Awards (ACAs): The fox television network created the ACAs in 2010 and also broadcasts the awards. The ACA Awards are voted on by fans, who choose their favorite country recordings, songs, and videos. Winners of the 2011 ACAs include Brad Paisley (Male Artist of the Year) and Carrie Underwood (Female Artist of the Year).

American Music Awards (AMAs): The AMA ceremony is broadcast each year on the ABC television network. TV host Dick Clark created the AMAs in 1973. The AMAs are awarded based on polls of the public. Taylor Swift was named Artist of the Year as well as top Female Country Artist at the 2011 AMAs.

Country Music Association (CMA) Awards: The Country Music Association was founded in 1958 and began hosting an award ceremony in 1967. CMA Awards are usually given out in the association's home base of Nashville. Taylor Swift won the 2011 CMA Entertainer of the Year award, while Jason Aldean's *My Kinda Party* took album of the year.

CMT Music Awards: Held in Nashville and broadcast live on Country Music Television, the CMTs are presented for music videos and TV performances. CMA wins are voted on by fans, who chose Taylor Swift as winner of the 2011 Video of the Year for "Mine." Miranda Lambert won Female Video of the Year for "The House That Built Me." Her husband, Blake Shelton, won in the male category for "Who Are You When I'm Not Looking."

Grammy Awards: The Grammys are the prestigious music awards given yearly by the National Academy of Recording Arts and Sciences. Lady Antebellum dominated the 2011 Grammys, winning Song of the Year and Record of the Year for "Need You Now" as well as Country Album, Country Song, and Country Performance by a Duo or Group with Vocals.

SOURCE NOTES

8   Colin Larkin, ed, The Encyclopedia of Popular Music, vol. 1 (New York: Oxford University Press, 2006), 39.

9   Paul Kingsbury and Alanna Nash, eds., Will the Circle Be Unbroken: Country Music in America (New York: Dorling Kindersley, 2006), 68.

10 Roy Acuff, quoted in Raymond Obstfeld and Sheila Burgener, eds., Twang! The Ultimate Book of Country Music Quotes (New York: Henry Holt and Co., 1997), 105.

18 Hank Williams, quoted in Colin Escott and Kira Florita, Hank Williams: Snapshots from the Lost Highway (Cambridge, MA: Da Capo Press, 2001), 124.

19 Bob Dylan, Chronicles: Volume One (New York: Simon and Schuster, 2004), 96.

21 John Morthland, The Best of Country Music (Garden City, NJ: Doubleday, 1984), 241.

26 Loretta Lynn, quoted in Raymond Obstfeld and Sheila Burgener, eds., Twang! The Ultimate Book of Country Music Quotes (New York: Henry Holt and Co., 1997), 49.

29 Buck Owens, liner notes to Don Rich, Country Pickin': The Don Rich Anthology (Sundazed, 2000).

30 Merle Haggard and Tom Carter, Merle Haggard's My House Full of Memories: For the Record (New York:

HarperEntertainment, 2002), 26.

33 Joe Nick Patoski, Willie Nelson: An Epic Life (New York: Little, Brown and Co., 2008), 220.

38 Lloyd Sachs, "Rodney Crowell Cashes In," Chicago Sun-Times, February, 11, 2001.

52 Geoffrey Himes, "A New Wave of Musicians Updates That Old-Time Sound," New York Times, November 5, 2006, http://www .nytimes.com/2006/11/05/arts/music/05hime .html?pagewanted=all (April 30, 2012).

52 Ibid.

SELECTED BIBLIOGRAPHY

Cooper, Daniel. Lefty Frizzell: The Honky-tonk Life of Country Music's Greatest Singer. Boston: Little, Brown and Co., 1995.

Davis, Mary, and Warren Zanes, eds. Waiting for a Train: Jimmie Rodgers's America. Burlington, MA: Rounder Books, 2009.

Dylan, Bob. Chronicles: Volume One. New York: Simon and Schuster, 2004.

Haggard, Merle, and Tom Carter. Merle Haggard's My House of Memories: For the Record. New York: Cliff Street Books, 1999.

Hemphill, Paul. Lovesick Blues: The Life of Hank Williams. New York: Viking, 2005.

———. The Nashville Sound: Bright Lights and Country Music. New York: Simon and Schuster, 1970.

Kingsbury, Paul, and Alanna Nash, eds. Will the Circle Be Unbroken: Country Music in America. New York: Dorling Kindersley, 2006.

Larkin, Colin, ed. The Encyclopedia of Popular Music. New York: Oxford University Press, 2006.

Malone, Bill C. Country Music, U.S.A.: A Fifty-Year History. Austin: American Folklore Society/University of Texas Press, 1968.

Malone, Bill C., and Judith McCulloh, eds. Stars of Country Music: Uncle Dave Macon to Johnny Rodriguez. Champaign: University of Illinois Press, 1975.

Morthland, John. The Best of Country Music. Garden City, NY: Doubleday, 1984.

Patoski, Joe Nick. Willie Nelson: An Epic Life. New York: Little, Brown and Co., 2008.

Streissguth, Michael. Johnny Cash: The Biography. Philadelphia: Da Capo Press, 2007.

Tosches, Nick. Country: The Biggest Music in America. New York: Stein and Day, 1977.

Willoughby, Larry. Texas Rhythm, Texas Rhyme: A Pictorial History of Texas Music. Austin: Texas Monthly Press, 1984.

Cash, Johnny. The Autobiography. New York: HarperOne 2003.

In *The Autobiography*, Johnny Cash reflects on his artistic triumphs, his marriages, and his spiritual beliefs. He also discusses his past addictions and parental failings. This book is a follow-up to Cash's 1986 memoir, *The Man in Black*.

Cash, Rosanne. *Composed: A Memoir*. New York: Viking, 2011.

Rosanne Cash jumps back and forth across time throughout this casual memoir. She recalls growing up with her single mother in California, far from her father, Johnny Cash; her relationship with him; and her beginnings as a singer-songwriter.

Chapman, Marshall. *They Came to Nashville*. Nashville: Vanderbilt University Press/Country Music Foundation Press, 2010.

Marshall Chapman is a quirky singer and songwriter with a successful career as a fiction writer. In this book, Chapman interviews fifteen country artists ranging from Willie Nelson to Miranda Lambert.

Gram Parsons: Fallen Angel. Directed by Gandulf Hennig. Produced by Gandulf Henning, Alfred Holighaus, Mark Cooper, and Mark Hagen. New York: Rhino, 2004.

Gandulf Hennig's documentary follows Gram Parson's transformation from restless Florida rich boy to country-rock legend. The film revolves around the bizarre plot to steal Parsons's body from his grave.

Grant, R. G. *The Great Depression*. Detroit: Lucent Books, 2005.

The Great Depression (1929–1942) was a period of economic hardship that shaped many famous country acts. With this book, readers can learn more about what caused the Depression and what life was like for the people who lived through it.

Green, Douglas. *Classic Country Singers*. Salt Lake City: Gibbs Smith, 2008.

This book has more information for young readers about country's great early performers. It also explains how different styles of country music changed over time.

Higgins, Melissa. *Taylor Swift: Country and Pop Superstar*. Minneapolis: ABDO Publishing, 2012.

Learn more about Taylor Swift's rise to the top of the country charts and her adventures in the spotlight.

Mazor, Barry. *Meeting Jimmie Rodgers: How America's Original Roots Music Hero Changed the Pop Sounds of a Century*. New York: Oxford University Press, 2009.

Nashville writer Mazor gives readers a look at the brief life and career of the Father of Country Music. Mazon outlines how Rodgers's yodels, storytelling, and lively sense of style would influence countless singers and songwriters.

McLeese, Don. *Dwight Yoakam: A Thousand Miles from Nowhere*. Austin: University of Texas Press, 2012.

This book takes a close look at the career of one of the all-time greatest crossover artists. After bursting on the Los Angeles punk-rock scene in the early eighties, Ohio native Yoakam became an arena-rock attraction without compromising his deep country sound.

Stuart, Marty. *Country Music: The Masters*. Naperville, IL: Sourcebooks MediaFusion, 2008.

Stuart is a country star who hosts his own show on the rural RFD-TV cable network. He drew upon his massive personal collection of photographs for this tribute to country greats he has known and played with. Stuart's book includes images of Johnny Cash, Bill Monroe, Lester Flatt, and more.

INDEX

ABOUT THE AUTHOR

Lloyd Sachs is a Chicago-based writer with extensive experience as a country, jazz, and pop critic. Author of the popular blog *jazzespress*, he was a senior editor and columnist for *No Depression*, the late and lamented alt-country/roots magazine. His cover profile of Rosanne Cash appeared in *The Best of No Depression: Writing about American Music*, published by the University of Texas Press. He has written for many major publications including *Rolling Stone*, *Downbeat*, the *Village Voice*, and the *Los Angeles Times*. He was the voice of *Sachs and the Cinema* on WXRT radio in Chicago and teaches *Reviewing the Arts* at Columbia College in Chicago.

PHOTO ACKNOWLEDGMENTS

The images in this book are used with the permission of: © Nigel Osbourne/Redferns/Getty Images, p. 1; © Brandy Sites/Dreamstime.com, p. 2; AP Photo/Gregory Bull, p. 3; © Rick Diamond/WireImage/Getty Images, p. 4; © BMI/Michael Ochs Archives/Getty Images, p. 5; © GAB Archive/Redferns/Getty Images, pp. 6, 14, 17; © Yale Joel/Time & Life Pictures/Getty Images, p. 7; © Michael Ochs Archives/Getty Images, pp. 8, 13 (right), 16 (bottom), 23, 28, 30; © Hulton Archive/Getty Images, pp. 9, 26; AP Photo, pp. 10, 19, 27 (right); © John Florea/Time & Life Pictures/Getty Images, p. 13 (left); © Frank Driggs/Michael Ochs Archives/Getty Images, p. 15; © Three Lions/Hulton Archive/Getty Images, p. 16 (top); © CBS-TV/The Kobal Collection/Art Resource, NY, p. 18; © Charles Trainor/Time & Life Pictures/Getty Images, p. 20; © Everett Collection/Rex USA, p. 21; © Bettmann/CORBIS, p. 22; © Keystone/Hulton Archive/Getty Images, p. 24; © Frank Driggs Collection/Archive Photos/Getty Images, p. 25; © David Redfern/Redferns/Getty Images, p. 27 (left); © Archive Photos/Getty Images, p. 29; AP Photo/Ric Feld, p. 32; © Bettmann/Corbis/AP Photo, p. 33; © Michael Putland/Hulton Archive/Getty Images, p. 34 (top); © Tom Wargacki/WireImage/Getty Images, p. 34 (bottom); © Gijsbert Hanekroot/Redferns/Getty Images, p. 35 (top); AP Photo/Mark Humphrey, pp. 35 (bottom), 40, 46; © Tony Korody/Sygma/CORBIS, p. 36 (left); © Robert Altman/Michael Ochs Archives/Getty Images, p. 36 (right); © Ebet Roberts/Redferns/Getty Images, p. 37; © Neal Preston/CORBIS, p. 39; © Joseph Cultice/CORBIS, p. 41; © Time & Life Pictures/Getty Images, p. 43; © Mick Hutson/Redferns/Getty Images, p. 44 (top); AP Photo/The Columbian, Troy Wayrynen, p. 44 (bottom); AP Photo/Mark Lennihan, p. 47; © AdMedia/WireImage/Getty Images, p. 48; © Jason Squires/WireImage/Getty Images, p. 49 (top); © Joey Foley/FilmMagic/Getty Images, p. 49 (bottom); AP Photo/Jim Cooper, p. 50 (top); © Kevin Mazur/WireImage/Getty Images, p. 50 (bottom); © Karl Walter/Getty Images, p. 51; AP Photo/John Russell, p. 52; © Paul Kane/Getty Images, p. 53; © Frederick Breedon IV/Getty Images, p. 54; © Jerod Harris/ACMA2011/Getty Images for ACM, p. 55.

Front cover: © iStockphoto.com/tirc83.

Main body text set in Arta Std Book 12/14
Typeface provided by International Typeface Corp